Mushkegowuk

New Orleans

From Mushkegowuk
to New Orleans:

A Mixed
Blood
Highway

Henry Kreisel Lecture Series

Henry Kreisel Lecture Series

From Mushkegowuk
to New Orleans:

A Mixed
Blood
Highway

Joseph
Boyden

Co-published by NeWest Press and the
Canadian Literature Centre | Centre de littérature canadienne

Library and Archives Canada Cataloguing in Publication

Boyden, Joseph, 1966–

From Mushkegowuk to New Orleans: a mixed blood highway / Joseph Boyden. (Henry Kreisel Lecture Series; 1)

ISBN 978-1-897126-29-5

1. Native peoples--Canada. 2. Native peoples--Canada--Social conditions. 3. New Orleans (La.)--Social conditions--21st century. I. Title. II. Series.

E78.C2B69 2008   971.004'97   C2008-901138-4

Editor for the Board: Diane Bessai
Cover design: Bob Robertson
Interior design: Bob Robertson and Lou Morin
Author photo: Stephanie Beeley

NeWest Press acknowledges the support of the Canada Council for the Arts, the Alberta Foundation for the Arts, and the Edmonton Arts Council for our publishing program. We also acknowledge the financial support of the Government of Canada through the Book Publishing Industry Development Program (BPIDP).

CANADIAN LITERATURE CENTRE
CENTRE DE LITTÉRATURE CANADIENNE

NeWest Press

8917 HUB Mall
Edmonton, Alberta T6G 2C5
780.492.9505
WWW.ARTS.UALBERTA.CA/CLC

201, 8540.109 Street
Edmonton, Alberta T6G 1E6
780.432.9427
WWW.NEWESTPRESS.COM

NeWest Press is committed to protecting the environment and to the responsible use of natural resources. This book is printed on 100% recycled, ancient forest-friendly paper.

1 2 3 4 5 11 10 09 08

Printed and bound in Canada

for Alootook Ipellie

Ever big wings you had. You're soaring now.

The Henry Kreisel Lecture Series

Henry Kreisel fled Nazi Austria at the age of sixteen and spent the next three years of his life in internment camps in England and eastern Canada. From such difficult national beginnings — as an "enemy alien" — he went on to become the University of Alberta's most distinguished working humanist. As a teacher of English and Comparative Literature, he was beloved for his capacity to change hearts and challenge minds. As Department Head and later Vice-President Academic, he was admired for his capacious open-mindedness — one of his many transformative accomplishments was to·introduce the first course in Canadian Literature to the University of Alberta. As a creative writer, he was read not only for his storytelling but for his ability to unsettle the cognitive landscape. His novels and stories brought another kind of global consciousness into the field of Canadian writing.

The University of Alberta's Canadian Literature Centre / Centre de littérature canadienne came into existence in 2006 with a mandate to bring book people together — teachers, students, scholars, collectors, librarians, authors, publishers, readers of every kind — and to foster a critical attitude that understands literature as a necessary participant in contemporary public debate. That mandate sits at the heart of the annual Henry Kreisel Lecture, which is here being published in collaboration with NeWest Press — a literary publishing house that Henry Kreisel himself helped to found over thirty years ago.

The Henry Kreisel Lectures celebrate the enduring presence of a scholar, teacher, and social critic who reached beyond the ivory tower and its disciplinary boundaries toward a wider community of minds. They celebrate the public lecture itself as a forum for open, inclusive, critical thinking. They celebrate the transformative capacity of literary language to foster in readers a commitment to social justice. And, they celebrate the inalienable contribution of imaginative writing to the project of social change.

Stephen Slemon

Director, Canadian Literature Centre
Professor, English and Film Studies
University of Alberta

January 2008

Introduction

Joseph Boyden's *Three Day Road* will be — if it is not already — a milestone in North American fiction. It is a brilliant ravelling of the essential threads of our great story, the meeting of the people of the 'Old World' with the people of Turtle Island, this continent as Aboriginal people name it. Boyden's tells this story through the fulcrum of conflict as European cultures reified it in the Great War that did not end all wars. In *Three Day Road*, two Anishinabe hunters turned Canadian snipers both war and observe war.

Why are Boyden and his first novel *Three Day Road* significant in Canadian literature in particular, and in literature and cross-cultural studies generally? Because in this novel his voice completes the Canadian story that David McFarlane began in *The Danger Tree*, that Frances Itani told in *Deafening*, and that the Blackfoot scholar James Dempsey documents in *Warriors of the King*. Our historians say that Canada became a nation in the Great War, but Boyden is the first to tell the whole Canadian story, the one that includes Aboriginal people.

Boyden's inauguration of the Henry Kreisel Lecture Series in the University of Alberta's ninety-ninth year is in itself telling. His invitation, his acceptance, and the lecture itself show the University's long awaited recognition of its Aboriginal heritage, as well as the breadth of its interdisciplinary reach. Native Studies, as an academic discipline, has multiple disciplinary roots. The University of Alberta has begun to nurture these, moving beyond the more common isolation of Aboriginal studies in small Arts departments. On the other hand, that it has taken ninety-nine years for the University to acknowledge the contributions Aboriginal people made and make to Alberta, and our place on Cree and Métis land, illustrates that the patience of Aboriginal people in this province is akin to the patience Boyden's snipers employ in *Three Day Road*.

Thus when Joseph Boyden accepted the invitation to inaugurate the Henry Kreisel Lecture Series, many of us were thrilled. It was an even greater pleasure for us to learn, when he delivered the lecture, that Boyden himself is the embodiment of the best of Canada and of the United States, his adopted home. *Three Day Road* is deeply grounded in the boreal forest of northern Ontario, the country and people of the James Bay Cree, as they are known to other Canadians. Boyden learned and learns his own Métis roots there, ancestry he traces through his mother. From his father, he inherited Irish and Scottish blood and the 'warrior' tradition he exposits so movingly in *Three Day Road*.

Boyden proved to be as authentic in person as his work on the page. He lectured passionately, relating Aboriginal people in Canada to poor African Americans, Whites, and Hispanics in post-Katrina New Orleans. He presented a challenge to the rest of us. What more can we ask of a contemporary author, thinker, speaker?

Ellen Bielawski

Dean, Native Studies
Adjunct Professor, English and Film Studies
University of Alberta

January 2008

From Mushkegowuk to New Orleans:
A Mixed Blood Highway

To be chosen as the inaugural speaker today is an honour, to say the least. A large part of me is still that child inside, the third youngest of eleven siblings who, when picked out of the crowd, always has that niggling question in the back of my mind: What did I do? It wasn't me! I swear. I've always felt more comfortable in the crowd, one face of many, quietly taking notes and creating stories.

I come by my writing honestly, I guess. I was born on a crisp Halloween morning in Canada forty years ago now. Converted to current American exchange rates, that puts me in my early thirties, tops. I don't feel forty. I'm not sure what you're supposed to feel like at forty. I notice my knees crack sometimes when I walk up stairs. The bits of grey have been duly noted by my wife, Amanda. Strangely enough, I was blond as a child, didn't inherit my mother's black hair until puberty, and so I have tried to convince my wife Amanda, and myself, that it isn't grey she's seeing in my hair; it's my locks trying to turn back to their original state. Sun bleached, I call it.

And what, you ask, does this have to do with Canadian literature? Why, everything! One of the great little bonuses of having written a successful novel is that I've been accepted into the ranks of other Canadian writers. I've run with the bulls in Pamplona with the brilliant Michael Winter after staying up all night drinking *calimocho*, a Basque concoction of red wine and Coca-Cola. Both Michael and I were convinced as the bulls stampeded by us that morning that we were going to die. Thankfully, we were too drunk to care in any real way. I've paddled Lake Kipawa with Margaret Atwood, watched her during a shore lunch talk with a gaggle of entranced female paddlers, stabbing her knife at them for emphasis. Margaret is a fantastic paddler, can go all day with the best of them. And, as I learned, like me Margaret will fall asleep in a teepee with complete strangers and snore just as loudly as any of us. I've hung out with Gord Downie in New Orleans, the man who is best known as the singer for the Tragically Hip, and to my mind, one of the great lyricists and poets our country has ever produced. Gord is whip smart and shy, a very different person from the madman on stage.

I share these little stories not to try to convince you — my audience — that I am indeed worthy of giving such an important lecture because, after all, I know some serious people! Really, I'm not trying to do that. All right, all right, maybe I am, just a little bit. I want you to think to yourselves, *Wow, Joseph knows some people. Therefore* (ergo, as you academics might be more prone to say), *he is worthwhile enough to give this lecture.* Which brings me back to my original point: a big part of me is still that shy little kid who doesn't like to be singled out. And so when Stephen Slemon contacted me months ago, asking if I'd consider this lecture, I had doubts. Doubt Number One: What could I possibly say that is worthwhile enough? Doubt Number Two: Aren't there dozens of other candidates far more fitting? Doubt Number Three: Edmonton in March? July or August, maybe.

The real reason, though, that I share a few little memories of my hanging with CanLit stars is that I've learned something over the last years. Canadian writers are really pretty normal. Boring, even. Think about it. We spend the majority of our day locked up in little rooms, writing in little notebooks or typing away on little laptops, desperately trying to present a world that is far more exciting than anything we've ever really experienced. And it struck me. Yes, I am worthy of giving this lecture. I'm relatively normal! I'm boring! So thank you, Stephen, for allowing me the chance to prove this to the good people of Edmonton.

Now, let me share something with you, an event that certainly didn't shape who I am so much as it had a great impact on my daily life in New Orleans, my adopted city:

◎

MAY, 2004 — The heat of the day has given way to an inky, balmy Louisiana night, our car windows rolled down as we speed, tires humming on pavement, along Bienville Street. In New Orleans, the killing heat of summer has already begun to present itself just as May has arrived. Amanda and me, we're coming home from a day at the fairgrounds, where Jazz Fest unfolds every spring. Many thousands come here for the music at this time each year, for the food, for a small bite of America's most original city. Our day has been one of the better Jazz

Fest days we'd experienced. And we've experienced many. Amanda accelerates through the yellow light at Carrollton, me bitching. "See," I say, almost gloating as she brakes hard on the quiet, dark road for a man in the middle of it, in front of us. "You keep speeding and cops'll get us."

The man in the street, black against the black asphalt and wearing a white T-shirt, looks up, looks into our head-lights. He's struggling, right there in our lane, with some-thing below him. Dropped groceries. A sack of something large. Not another car or person in sight, just Amanda and me and this man ahead. We stop in front of him. He's not a man at all, but a teen, his eyes wide open, caught in some embarrassing act, staring into our lights. It's not dropped groceries he's struggling with, we see, but another young man sitting down in the road.

We are close enough to see blood on the sitter's blue shirt. The young one on top drags his charge out of our way to the curb. Amanda pulls up beside the two, and I'm going to ask them if they're all right, if they need some help. The kid on the ground must be drunk. He's fallen on the road, head lolling, and his friend is helping him get out of our way, keeping him safe from the white, too-fast drivers.

What happens next, it happens in seconds. But to this day it plays out in my head like a lifetime. My arm hangs out the window, close enough to reach and touch these two young men. I am about to open my mouth when I see that the standing teen has a pistol in his hand. He looks at me, eyes cold now, and begins to raise the gun toward us. I shout to Amanda, "He's got a gun! Drivedrivedrive!" In the very instant she peels away, I see the kid change his mind, lower the gun. He points it at the head of the one below him and pulls the trigger. I watch the barrel flash, hear the gun pop. Doesn't sound loud at all. He turns then and runs, fast as he can, down a side street.

Not half a block away, I scream, "Stopstopstop!" Amanda doesn't want to. I scream again. She does. "I saw which way he went," I shout, opening the door and bolting. "No!" Amanda panics. I go, running, then stopping, worried about the return of the shooter. I barely hear Amanda yelling into the row of dark houses, "Call 911! Call 911!" I stare down the side street, look to see if the shooter will come back. Will kill me. I run to the man on the ground. He looks so small. He lies on his side, fetal position, eyes staring at the dirty blacktop. He panics when I approach. He whines like a baby with a stomachache, begins to hyperventilate when I kneel. "I'm not him," I whisper. "It's OK."

I stroke his hair, and he calms. His whine becomes a moan. He stares out at the road, waiting. I sit down and put his head on my lap. I stroke his head like he's my child. "It's OK. You're going to be OK." I hum to cover his moan, to relax him. He's bleeding out, I see, his blue shirt soaked black in the street light, blood running out of him and puddling by the curb. He's shot in the chest. I consider mouth-to-mouth, but only for a second. He's dying, and there's nothing anyone can do about it. Only then do I see the bullet hole, neat and round, in his cheek. I stroke his head and whisper, "You're OK. You're going to be OK. Just breathe." I think he takes some solace in my words. The panic has turned to resolve. To calm. I hum some more, continue stroking his head. His short black hair is wiry, greasy. He's as thin as my son, who will be fourteen next month. But this one on the ground, bleeding on me, he's clearly a few years older. His breathing slows. "You're going to be OK.

Just breathe," I whisper, I hum, as his eyes glass over and he dies in my lap.

Now, consider this next story I will share with you, an event fourteen years earlier, almost to the day, a story that *has* in many ways shaped who I am:

◎

TORONTO, MAY, 1990 — We're stuck in rush hour traffic at eight-thirty AM on Sheppard Avenue in North York. She turned nineteen last month. I am twenty-three, won't meet Amanda for another two years.

We are in the back seat of a Buick Skylark. She's sprawled on the seat, naked. I crouch awkwardly between her spread legs. She's screaming. Her mother, who's driving, screams as well. I look up for a moment, out the window, and see the shocked expression of a woman staring back at me from another car.

Our car inches forward, horn blaring, and I look back down. Blood. Lots of it on the seat. That will never come out, I think. Upholstery is ruined. White noise in my head like a TV that's set to a blank station at full volume. I'm sure this girl is dying. She screams more. A blood smeared round lump pushes out from her body. The head of my child. She yelps, and the lump pushes out further.

My eyes watch all of this unfold, my brain numb with horror. But my hands, they are calm and steady. The hands of my long-dead surgeon father. The blood smeared mass spits out fast from her body, and my hands catch it and stop it from slipping onto the floor.

The little thing is long and skinny. It's blue in the harsh morning light. The umbilical cord is wrapped tightly about its neck. It doesn't move, doesn't cry, doesn't breathe. I see all of this, am shocked to blankness to see all of this. But the hands, they work steadily, unwinding the umbilical cord. The body is slippery. Don't drop it.

Now it begins to gasp a little, but something still prevents it from drawing breath. The pointer finger of my left hand prods the tiny mouth open, scoops out bile and goo. The hands turn the baby onto its stomach. While the right hand cradles it, the left hand gives a quick slap to the tiny rump. The baby gasps, begins to draw in more breath, bleats like a lamb. The bleats turn into wails. The blue skin begins to turn pink.

I watch as one hand gently wipes some blood from the child. The other hand makes a nest of the mother's robe on her puffed stomach. Both hands lay the baby gently in the robe to keep it warm. The baby screams full-fledged now, its lungs clear and obviously strong. Its mother lies back with eyes closed, breathing easier, passed out. The new grandmother honks her way through traffic and speeds into the emergency room entrance of North York General. I haven't even noticed if my child is a boy or a girl.

We settle, two days later, on the name Jacob. Despite family protests on both sides, I decide that his middle name will be Buick. I like to drive him through the dark streets of my neighbourhood at night. He is loud, healthy, and only calms each evening to the hum of car tires on pavement.

And so maybe these two stories, both absolutely true, serve as metaphors for my life thus far. Maybe. But one thing I have learned as a writer is not to push a metaphor too far. What is the fun in setting something up in word pictures only to go ahead and explain it? Let the reader, the listener decide.

Another story, this one geographical, a love story about place, and a love story about two people, if you will.

◎

I first crossed the Lake Pontchartrain Causeway, consisting of two parallel bridges that are the longest in the world, and entered into the city of New Orleans, in July, 1988. I was travelling with friends from South Carolina, was a roadie for their punk rock band. We were on a tour of America, riding in a battered Chevy van and living a true hand-to-mouth existence. If shows were cancelled, which they were, we didn't eat that day. If the van broke down, which it did, we didn't eat that day. I recommend to anyone who is finding it difficult to lose a few pounds, to become a roadie for a punk rock band.

But we knew how to have fun. We were young and alive! We were full of Jack Kerouac and full of excitement for what the next town, the next city, the next few miles would bring us. We'd gotten crappy tattoos together in LA, we wrestled in the salt flats of Utah, we played with the Dead Kennedys in Berkeley. And then there was New Orleans. In July. Like stepping into the mouth of an overheated dog. Nights a touch cooler when all the people came out. When the danger came out. My first experience in a city of trying to get used to the sound of random gunfire. We stayed with a friend, Jay, an artist who lived in part of an old mansion with sixteen foot high ceilings and three dogs. He took us to Uptown blues clubs, to downtown cheap restaurants. He showed us the city, where to find happy hour prices at five in the morning. I fell in love with the living, breathing history that place, where Buddy Bolden first played a music called jazz at the Treme, where the Mississippi River curves slow like a crescent, where the antebellum architecture, the live oak lined avenues, the streetcars clanging down St. Charles that looked, and probably were, from the forties, they all led to the same place. Decadence. Even on a shoestring. Every young man's dream. The sense of lurking danger down rough looking blocks. It is a city easy to fall in love with.

And so eventually I decided to move there. I returned home with that sense of obligation that has always followed me around like an unwanted pet, and finished my undergrad degree at York University. But still, The City That Care Forgot called, and I spent all my time working jobs and scraping together enough cash to return for a week, two weeks.

Eventually, I came to the decision to apply to graduate school. And I applied to only one place. The University of New Orleans, for an MFA degree in fiction. Somehow, I got accepted. In August of 1992, having saved up for a year, I said goodbye to my family and drove down on my motorcycle with only what I could carry, just as a hurricane was bearing down on New Orleans. The hurricane took a last minute turn and side-swiped us. Minimal damage. A lot of hurricane parties. I didn't ever flee a hurricane until Ivan came the year before Katrina. My wife Amanda and me, we ran.

Amanda. I met her our first day of classes. She'd moved down from St. Louis to study in the same program as me. I won't go into the scandalous details, but let's just say that she moved down from St. Louis with a boyfriend, and I had come down to move in with a girlfriend. Within a year, destiny had made its demands, and within a few years we were married, in October 2005, during our last semester of school.

Amanda and I were married in an outdoor ceremony in Audubon Park on a gorgeous sunny afternoon, under a giant oak tree the locals call the Tree of Life. The Tree of Life is massive. One hundred people can rest comfortably on its limbs. A Jesuit priest and an Ojibwa healer helped to marry us. Yes, our wedding ceremony was a bit of an anomaly, just like our city. A cello played as we walked down the grassy aisle, a brass band and a blues band rocked the reception. As crazy as this sounds, five days before the wedding, a hurricane was heading right for us, adding considerably to our prenuptial stress. This one had a pretty name. Hurricane Opal. Family was on the way from Canada, from all over America, straight into the jaws of a potential beast. But as always, at the last minute it veered away, knocking out Pensacola, delivering us sunshine and cool breezes. New Orleans was blessed. We were convinced.

As blessed as we once thought this city was, it is a city that can be horribly cruel. People who have lived here for any amount of time talk about a love/hate relationship with New Orleans. A city easy to fall in love with, but once you live there for any amount of time the social and economic and racial ills start bubbling up from the storm drains and before you know it, you are surrounded. It's a tough place to live in. Often, it feels like the loose knit gangs that roam the streets control the city. Violence, murderous violence, is an everyday occurrence. And I believe that this violence stems from poverty. New Orleans is terribly poor. People don't call it a banana republic for nothing. A seemingly carefree and uncaring bourgeoisie on St. Charles Avenue uptown tsk-tsking at the dangers, the anarchy on lesser streets.

And so, soon after our marriage, Amanda and I moved. I took her back to my country, to my home, where we stayed for a few years before the addiction that is New Orleans could no longer be denied.

Just one more love story, this one geographical as well, but a different type of love story:

◎

The Moose River's mouth is so wide that if you were on the big water of James Bay searching for it, you'd think it wasn't a river at all but a great inlet. Dangerous waters there. Wind can whip up the shallow bay into monster waves. Strong currents, but it's the waves that have drowned so many. Water, like my son, shows its anger on the surface. This is the place that has inspired my writing, but it is more than that. This place that I love can be dangerous, but it is more than that, too.

My son and I, we like it better on the river than on the bay. Too many ghosts out on the big water. Don't get me wrong. Plenty of ghosts on the river, too. But they never seemed as aggressive as the ones out there. You can appease the river ghosts easier with a sprinkle of tobacco and a few whispered prayers. You get out on the big water in a storm and a carton of Player's isn't going to help. And so, my son and I, we stay to the rivers.

Start at the mouth and follow the Moose by travelling against its strong current, and in about six or seven miles you will hit Moosonee on the right and Moose Factory on the left. Moosonee is accessible only by train, Moose

Factory by freighter canoe in summer and ice road in winter. I've heard visitors call Moosonee *hardscrabble*, and Moose Factory *a shining example of the reserve system*. Go there, I urge you. Decide for yourself.

Travel this river with my son and me, push against the current, heading south past the hydro wires and on to the Kwetabohigan Rapids. Long, rolling water dotted with submerged boulders. Good paddling, just tricky enough to keep your heart beating fast. You look down and all you see is black, the brown shoulders of big rocks just below flashing by and threatening to flip your canoe.

Past the Kwetabohigans are the sandy shores of Negobau Islands. The river here is wide. Old campgrounds on the heads of the islands that go back more generations than I want to count. On a canoe trip once, my son and I wandered the beaches and he bent down to find an eagle feather lying there. A gift for him. Good energy on those islands, a place of rest and comfort for ancestor travellers.

A few miles past, if you head left toward the sound of the crashing water, you find the Allan Rapids. This is where the Abitibi pours into the Moose. Good rapids that challenge even the best paddlers. If you're coming down them, stay to the extreme left, hugging the sharp cliffs of the shore that rise up from the mist.

Push south in the calmer water, past the islands so big they look like mainland. Sturgeon as large as a man nudge rocks below you, turning them over with their snub noses, sucking up crayfish. The black spruce and poplar and aspen are thick along the shores. The water is shallow despite the river's girth. Otter Rapids Generating Station, dozens of miles south, upriver, is part of the reason, opening its mouth once a day to ease the built up tension behind its concrete, causing the river to rise and settle as if it is governed by tides. Above, ospreys glide and watch.

Twenty miles now of rock lead up to bush. Drinking creeks spill into the river, beavers dam up the bigger creeks; moose and fox and marten and wolves on the land, pickerel and pike and sturgeon in the water. Pulp mills and loggers, they want this place. Well, not all of it. Just the land by the rivers, where the choice trees grow. The loggers, they know that if they are to harvest the trees by the rivers and creeks they will create mass erosion that will kill off the fish, and then the land animals who hunt them. But they want it still. And they say they will get it from the Cree.

My friend William's camp, where the Onakawana slips into the Abitibi, is the most magical place I know. A couple of cabins on a ridge above the river where you can watch the endless flow of water below, the forest and the river giving us what we need to survive. The spring breakup thunders and sometimes sends the ice water so high it floods the camp. In autumn, we hunt moose grazing red willow on the shores. In spring, after spawn, we fish for pickerel and pike that feed all of us. Enough for us to bring back gifts of thick fillets to elders in Moosonee and Moose Factory. In summer, my son and I paddle from William's camp with the current, paddle to friends in the north. In winter, we snowmobile up and down the frozen back of the river between William's camp and the Bay.

This stretch of water between James Bay and the Onakawana is where I bring my son when we need to reconnect again. When the trouble of his teenage years threatens to unground him, and me. There's magic in this stretch of river. Magic on the shores. No one else around but us. This place, it belongs to no one, to everyone. To those who respect it. These rivers, and the lowlands around it, are part of Mushkegowuk, the Moose Cree homeland. This magic, it passes through us, those who own nothing and everything. It has become a part of my son, and of me.

And so these are the two halves of my life so far. It was once pointed out to me that both of these places are extremes, of themselves and to one another. Extremes in landscape and geography and temperature, extremes in lifestyle and culture, extremes in experience. It was also once pointed out to me that a person who craves such extremes might very well be mentally unsound. If that is the case, I too come by this honestly.

My father was studying medicine in Vienna in the 1930s when he witnessed the rise of Nazism. He went home to Canada knowing what approached on the horizon as surely as if it were bad weather. He joined the Canadian Expeditionary Force on 3 September 1939, the first day war was declared, and went on to serve as a front line doctor in Africa and Europe. My father was of mixed descent, mostly Irish, some Dutch, some Nipmuck Indian from Massachusetts. A North American, a Canadian whose family stretched back many generations. My father's claim to fame is one he rarely spoke of. He became the British Empire's most highly decorated medical officer in the Second World War. His military title was Lt. Colonel Raymond Wilfrid Boyden, DSO, CD, MD.

A retired military man by the name of General Brown, who is still alive today, once pointed out to my oldest brother, a former military man as well, that medical officers aren't supposed to receive DSOs, Distinguished Service Orders. Those are saved for fighting men in combat roles. When my brother asked how this had come about, General

Brown related a story my father never spoke of with any of his children. The general told my brother that my father had actually been awarded the Victoria Cross. In early 1945, while in Rome, my father stayed up all night drinking with some buddies. As he stumbled out into the purple dawn, he came across a British general responsible for sending a number of my father's troops into a stupid and deadly engagement that killed many of them. Angry, drunken words were spoken, fists flew, and my father punched out a general and lost a VC.

Before you ask yourself what in the world this has to do with anything, let me counter by saying that I firmly believe that one can't talk about a sense of place without acknowledging where one comes from. This is a strong tradition with both the Irish and the Ojibwa.

My father ingrained in all of us a vital sense of social justice. He was a doctor who would take for payment what a patient could afford. Many of my father's patients were immigrants new to this country who still raised animals for food. Consequently, I was raised with a backyard full of ducks, rabbits, lambs, and goats. But my father could never bring himself to slaughter any of these pets. I think he'd seen enough killing for many lifetimes. Our menagerie grew and shrank, according to nature.

My mother was much younger than my father, was a schoolteacher when she met him, and returned to teaching when he died in order to support my siblings and me. My mother's family is Scottish and Métis, and my mother made all of our meals, raised all of us single-handed for many years, even sewed all of our clothes until she had to return to teaching. I grew up wearing what might not have been the height of fashion, but at least I matched my brothers and sisters. It was very hard at times wearing a plaid suit with a Dutch boy haircut. But it helped to foster a sense of individualism, I guess. My mother's still alive, lives in northern Ontario on the land she loves.

And so I have my father's wanderlust and my mother's work ethic and their collective strong beliefs that social justice must exist if we as humans must exist. I am the product of these two very different people, a card carrying member of the Métis Nation who lives between Northern Ontario and Southern Louisiana.

My father saw the rise of something more than un-healthy, something inherently inhuman back in the 1930s. And to some lesser degree, I myself see bad weather on the near horizon, weather that already affects us and will only get worse unless we act soon. Having lived in the US since before 9/11, I acutely feel the difference in tempera-ture in America. It's become a place far less open-minded, a land where the erosion of civil rights is assumed to be the cost of staying safe. Safe from terrorists and inflation and illegal immigrants.

My thinking is nothing new, or even anything especially provocative. Where else in the world can most any scientist state beyond a shadow of a doubt that global warming is a clear and imminent threat and yet the federal government, run by men with strong ties to the oil industry, refuse to openly recognize this? Where else in the world can a cor-poration from which the Vice-President of the country still receives residuals score non-competitive government con-tracts in the billions? Where else in the world can a city be drowned and half its population — coming on two years later — still be unable to return home? Not a lot to return home to, unless you consider a skyrocketing murder rate as bad as it was before Katrina to be return to normalcy.

And this is not to say our country, Canada, is perfect. By any means. Some politicians have tried hard — continue to try hard — to make their vision of Canada one far too similar to that of the US. A mini-me of America, if you will. As someone who has lived there, all I can say is ... why? Now why would you want to do that? Please, go live there for a while. Work in a state-run university in the second poorest state in the union, in a city where the average citizen can't afford medical insurance and where the only state run hospital in the city was destroyed by Katrina and had its funding pulled. In a city where generations of poverty and racism and denial and incompetence and graft have born an underclass of angry and desperate young people who have no future.

And yet I still live there. Amanda and I talked about it. A lot. Should we move somewhere safer? Should we move back to Canada? We realize moving now is quitting, is giving up on the place that saw some of our biggest dreams come to life, that was a big part of the reason for them coming to life. Possibly the only statement of the current president's that I can agree with, even if it is in a completely different context, is that we can't cut and run. Failure of New Orleans is not an option. And so I will continue to split my life between the two places that I love.

It's very easy for us to be all smug and content when looking to our southern neighbour. Really easy, for mostly good reasons. And yet, what I am going to share is no big secret among average Canadians. And it too is nothing especially insightful or even provocative. Just as New Orleans is an example of the system failed, of injustice of massive proportions, of promises broken and of a city, a place, that care forgot, so are many of our reserves right here in Canada. Me, I can only speak for the ones that I've visited, the ones that I lived in and got to know. And so I will speak of Northern Ontario reserves, places like Kashechewan and Fort Albany and Attawapiskat, places like Peguis and Wasauksing.

I've been lucky enough to spend a lot of time on the isolated reserves of the far north of Ontario. I've taught communications on the James Bay coast for Northern College, but my teaching life there ironically became a life of learning. These reserves are ancient cultures trying to find their way in a continually encroaching modern era. Kids will return from the goose and the moose hunt only to log online and enter chat rooms with other kids from all over the world. Their parents still speak Cree as their first language and the younger ones, more and more, only speak English. Alcohol abuse and drug abuse continue to erode families and feed violence. It was briefly reported by *The Globe and Mail* a couple of months ago that in a Kashechewan community of about nine-hundred, twenty-one youths had attempted suicide in a thirty day period. You also might remember Kashechewan as being the reserve where an E. coli outbreak was imminent due to a tainted drinking water supply.

The government's stand remains the same: when the press uncovers a potential scandal, throw enough money at the problem to try to temporarily quell it, to stave off the scandal waiting to happen for just a little longer. Once again this spring, the ice buildup north of Kash, much of it caused by poor engineering of levees, of all things, will threaten to flood the community and send the people flee-ing south to Timmins and Moosonee to languish while their homes fill with water that destroys their few possessions. Sound familiar?

As troubled and desperate as Kashechewan and many of these northern communities sound, and often are, to spend any time there is to see another side as well. I've never met a people who better understand the importance of humour. To laugh when you are hurting is a simple but undeniable way to make what might seem impossible and cruel circumstances livable. When I first began travelling to northern communities, I was concerned I'd be treated as an outsider, an interloper. But my fears were banished immediately. The smile of a kookum, a grandmother, as I walk by her on the dusty street is the most welcoming smile I've ever experienced. The smile is real, the eyes scrunched, questioning. "And what are you doing here? Welcome." Children playing street hockey beg you to be the goalie so they can test their best moves on you, laughing the whole time as they neatly slip the tennis ball past you and into the net. People your age invite you over for dinner and you play with their kids who treat you like a Jungle Gym. Despite astronomical unemployment and poverty, there is still a magic in Kashechewan and similar communities. I think this magic has always been there. But magic is intangible, something not easily explained in a newspaper article attempting to uncover some hostile and ugly realities.

Clearly, there is no simple answer to the question, "What is wrong in these communities, and how do we right it?" I think there is truth in the theory that the reserve system is inherently set up to make individuals fail, or to not allow young people to succeed. In many ways, many of the reserves in our country are the housing projects of America, rural instead of urban, but faced with the same crippling poverty, and the violence, addiction, and broken families that poverty creates.

And I am convinced that the residential school system that was forced onto the Native population of Canada for many generations is one of the roots of the current situation. At around the beginning of the 20TH Century, the federal government began the practice of taking children away from their parents in order to educate them. This practice removed the children from their parents' arms and placed them in absolutely foreign institutions, usually run by religiously affiliated organizations. Overwhelmingly, children were banned from speaking their own language, practicing their own religion, learning their culture's significance, or seeing their parents for nine or ten months of the year. The children were given western haircuts, western clothes, and indoctrinated with western thinking. The idea behind this was simple: remove the Indian from the Indian, and in this way integrate the native population into the white mainstream. And in those most vulnerable years, the teen years, those children were sent back home, no longer knowing their language, their religion, their land, their customs, or their parents. Generation after generation was taught who our prime ministers were, how to say the Lord's Prayer, how to apply simple mathematics, and how to speak English. But they no longer knew their parents, and often, and most importantly, how to be a parent. This skill can only be taught through being reared by one.

Obviously now we can see the inherent flaws of this system. But what has come to the surface in the federal courts in this land over the last couple of decades, and what the native population in Canada has tried to come to terms with for generations, is a far more troubling reality. A reality of institutional abuse: physical, mental, and sexual. And this abuse was rampant, not just happening in isolated pockets. What often surprises many Canadians is that the residential school system went full steam ahead until 1975, only thirty-two years ago. What we are seeing now, I believe, is the fallout of an incredibly short-sighted, cruel, and inhumane system. The effects of this system, forced upon a whole population against their will, will take generations to undo. And so, we're in it for the long run, people.

Having fallen in love with the far north of Ontario and the far south of Louisiana, two places so geographically removed and so different in many ways, I can't help but have noticed striking similarities. Flying into either place in summer, you will notice from above that muskeg and bayous look startlingly similar, pockets of land surrounded by marsh, the gulf of a great ocean sparkling in the distance, a similar biosphere teeming with life, sturgeon feeding on crayfish in the rivers, beavers working diligently as only beavers can, black spruce on the shores in the north, cypress in the south. While in the winter months temperature differences are extreme, in the summer months the same mosquitoes come to life and indigenous populations in both places live off the land in much the same way they have for thousands of years.

But it's the social similarities of two very different populations that is most striking to me, two cultures that have suffered abuses and been beaten down for years and act surprisingly the same: both have a strong sense of racial identity, the same disdain for authority, a vibrant and rebellious youth movement expressing itself through spoken word and rap. Two cultures separated by a continent that share the endemic problems that stem from abject poverty — violence, substance abuse, broken families — but who refuse to be defined by them. A re-emergence of cultural identity in youth that is expressed in art and music and fashion. One striking similarity, for me, is a subculture in New Orleans loosely termed Mardi Gras Indians, mixed race blacks who are the descendants of runaway slaves taken in by the Aboriginal population of South Louisiana who today still dress on special occasions in home sewn outfits of feathers and beads and parade through the city, celebrating their unique heritage.

Just as in Aboriginal Canada, where the system has failed its people so completely, in New Orleans there is the same grassroots desire for self-government, for self rule. And a self-righteous undertone exists in both countries, blaming the people who have been victimized and swept aside for so long for their own problems. Why do you live in a place prone to flooding, to violence and addiction? Why don't you just move? As if the simple act of picking up and leaving New Orleans or Kashechewan is a viable option, as if the idea of leaving the place where you were born and that you love despite its problems is an option. As if these two populations have brought all of these problems upon themselves. And I am beginning to hear some of the same words being expressed in these very different, and yet similar, communities. Words that speak about independence, even address the possibility of secession; I see a growing movement. Both the native population of Canada and the population of South Louisiana sit upon vast natural resources from which they don't benefit. Both populations are unfairly blamed for their own circumstances, both populations are treated as bastard children that nobody wants to recognize.

It might surprise some that many people in both communities (and here I admittedly generalize the Aboriginal population in Canada as a loosely knit community facing many of the same situations) are sick of being viewed by the greater population as lazy, as drunks, as more than happy to sit back and collect welfare cheques, are sick of being viewed in the most general and racist and bigoted of terms as responsible for their current situation and doing nothing to fix it. Many in both communities are angry when natural disasters like flooding, or man-made disasters like E. coli outbreaks, are blamed on us. These two diverse populations inherently understand that we've received the short end of the stick and are blamed for still grasping for it.

All of this got me thinking. When a significant population is continually treated so poorly, often for circumstances not of their doing, that population reaches a boiling point, and a grassroots revolution is born, defined by a manifesto. And so maybe it is time for two diverse but distinct populations to band together, the Aboriginal in Canada, and the mixed race population of New Orleans. Despite certain obvious differences, we share far more similarities, one of which is the fact that our governments have continually let us down, and the bigger population around us doesn't give a damn. And so it is time for us to unite and to demand that certain inalienable rights be recognized. It is time to declare independence from North America, to shake off the chains of two foreign governments who, while stealing from us with the left hand, offer us a mere pittance of our value with the right.

I will title my manifesto *If At First You Don't Secede, Try, Try Again*, and, in part, it will go something like this:

When in the course of events, human and otherwise, it becomes necessary for two different but equal populations and people to break the political chains which have bound them to others, and to assume among the powers of the earth, the separate and equal place to which the Laws of Nature entitle them, a half-hearted respect for the opinions of the rest of the world requires that these two different but equal populations should declare the causes which impel them to separation.

We hold these truths to be as self-evident as the slurs of drunken and lazy that have been hurled at our two populations for too long: that neither New Orleans nor the hundreds of reserves across Canada were created equal, that this city and these reserves have been endowed by nature with certain obvious cultural advantages, that among these are a Laissez-faire disposition, an Innate Ability to create universally unrivalled music and cuisine, and the Resilience that only Indians have tempered, Mardi Gras Indians or otherwise.

Whenever a government ignores our mutual plight, exploits our resources and gives a mere pittance back, subjects our peoples to massive injustice and even goes so far as to pimp us out in motion pictures, allowing us to be so wrongly represented in feature films such as *Dances with Wolves* or *The Big Easy*, when clearly we are not at all like that, it is the right of the People to alter or abolish these governments, and to institute a new government laying its foundation on such principles as will secure our natural advantages.

Such has been the patient suffering of New Orleans and of the reserves of Canada, and such is now the necessity which constrains us to change our former systems of government. The history of North America is a history of repeated injuries and usurpations, all having in direct Object the establishment of an absolute tyranny over this city and these reserves.

To prove this, let a few facts be submitted to an uncaring world:

She (being the mutual governments of Canada and the us) has plundered our natural resources and ravaged our forests and our coasts, our muskeg and our marshes.

She has cut off trade with many of our natural allies, such as Cuba and Venezuela in the south, and France and Holland in the east.

She has endeavoured to lure invaders to our frontiers, the carpetbagger Wal-Mart in the South, the Northern Store in the north, both of which are characterized by their cheap products, long checkout lines, ridiculously expensive and wilted fruits and vegetables, and poor customer service.

She has for years dumped her trash, sewage, toxic waste and other refuse into the Mississippi River in the south, the Moose and Albany Rivers in the north, with the full knowledge that all would eventually pass through the city of New Orleans and the reserves of Canada and in many cases, enter our water supply.

She has continually sent us her carpetbaggers, but rarely accepted ours.

She has stolen jazz from us in the south, and Aboriginal drumming and singing in the north, and claimed both as Her sole indigenous art forms.

She has continuously misrepresented our dialect and our customs in film and made-for-TV movies, portraying the cultural habits of Indians as rudimentary, and the speech of New Orleanians as twangy Texan or Bible belt cracker.

She has come to New Orleans and worn Mardi Gras beads when it was not Carnival season and believed that wearing such beads gave Her complete licence to act like a barbaric imbecile. She has come to our northern powwows and treated them as quaint outdated displays geared for Her enjoyment.

In almost every stage of these Oppressions, Transgressions, Impositions, and Nuisances we have petitioned for Redress in the humblest terms of which we are capable. Our repeated petitions have only been answered by repeated injury.

We, therefore, in General Congress, Assembled, appealing to the Supreme Judge, the Gitchi Manitou of the world, for the rectitude of our intentions, do, in the name of, and by the Authority of, the relatively good people of New Orleans and Indigenous Canada, as solemnly as we can, publish and declare That New Orleans and Indigenous Canada are, and of Right ought to be, Free and Independent and allowed to create a loose and mutually beneficial Union relying on our massive natural resources and similar cultures and circumstances, that we are to be absolved from all allegiance to North America, that all political connection between us and North America be totally dissolved, and that as a Free and Loosely Knit and Independent Nation, we have full power to levy war, conclude peace, contract alliances, establish Commerce, determine our own holidays, identify our own Heroes, and to do all other Acts and Things we damn well please.

Meegwetch. Thank you.

◎

A special *Meegwetch* to Jackson Moss
for inspiring my manifesto.

◎

About the author

Joseph Boyden is a member of the Ontario Woodland Métis. His first collection of stories, *Born With A Tooth*, was shortlisted for the Upper Canada Writers' Craft Award and has been published in Canada and France. His debut novel, *Three Day Road*, is an international bestseller and has been published in thirteen languages. The first novel to be translated into Cree, it has received numerous awards in Canada and abroad, including the Roger's Writers' Trust Prize. Joseph splits his time between Moosonee (or James Bay Lowlands) and New Orleans. He and his wife, novelist Amanda Boyden, are both currently writers-in-residence at the University of New Orleans.

About the Canadian Literature Centre

The Canadian Literature Centre | Centre de littérature canadienne was established at the University of Alberta in 2006. As the western hub of the Canadian literary community, it brings together researchers, authors, publishers, collectors, and the reading public. The Centre aims to promote literary research—in both English and French—of all genres, languages, and regions of the country, and to foster public interest in Canadian literature with a view to enhancing an understanding of the richness and diversity of Canada's written culture.